WELLS: A FAIR PLACE

Wells: A Fair Place

Richard Green

redcliffe

First published in 2001 by Redcliffe Press Ltd.,
81g Pembroke Road, Bristol BS8 3EA

Tele: 0117 9737207

© Richard Green

ISBN 1 900178 58 3

British Library Cataloguing in Publication Data
A catalogue record for this book is available from
The British Library

Typeset by Mayhew Typesetting, Rhayader, Powys
and printed by Hackman Print, Tonypandy

Contents

Foreword

Not everyone who visits the market and even the fair realises that a long and rich history lies behind them. This book paints vivid pictures of the past. A story which mentions kings, bishops, the Black Death, the great wars, Buffalo Bill, Teddy boys, Bill Moore's boxing booth is a story of the people through 800 years winning rights to hold the market and the fairs which continue to this day. It is also a story which is properly more interested in the market stall-holders and the families who kept the tradition of the fairs alive.

We need to know the history of our city. It is colourful and fascinating, and provides a representation of the centuries in the city, with the Market Place, the Cathedral, and the Bishop's Palace at its centre. It shows also that the city is at its best when councils, markets, fairs and church work together for the benefit of the residents, commerce and visitors. As we look back to our medieval forebears and marvel, it gives pause for thought as to how the marketeers and fairground performers of those days would react to Wells in the Third Millennium after Christ. This book is about the ongoing community and strengthens the sense of tradition and belonging. The city is all the more precious for these resilient contributions to its identity. May it thrive for the next 1,000 years.

The Bishop of Bath and Wells, March 2001
The Right Reverend James Thompson

Introduction

This book is a tribute to the market traders and travelling showmen and their families, for without them there would be no 800th anniversary of the first Royal Charter. As these pages show, there have been many ups and downs in their trade and commerce, and many threats to their long-standing traditions.

As a Wellensian, I am proud to have compiled this book; even more so, meeting and getting involved with the real people who uphold the rights of the Charter, the market traders and families of the showmen.

Whatever the weather, whatever the economic outlook, both the market traders and the showmen have, against whatever obstacles in their path, such as higher rents, always remained resilient and philosophical. Their religious heritage and loyalty to tradition are undeniable, and their close-knit family community is something we can all aspire to.

I feel honoured to have been given an insight into our twice-weekly and twice-yearly events, and hope that this evocation of the commodities, the livestock, the amusements and the religious and civic background will help give a better understanding of our last remaining, real-life traditions.

Richard Green, May 2001.

Acknowledgements

This book would not have been possible without the help and encouragement of many people, to whom I express my sincere thanks:

Caroline Bagias, Bodleian Library, Oxford, Lawrence Brice, Bristol Record Office, David Bromwich, Councillor Chris Clarke, Heather Clay, Sarah Curnow, Cheryl and Richard Carter, Chewton Mendip School, City of Wells Council, Billy Cole, Alf Cooper, Jane Doble, Nancy Dodd, Edward Dyer, Fairground Association of Great Britain, Fairground Society, Ivy Flagg, Bob Freebury, Paul Fry, Fred Gibbons, Jean Gray, Guildhall Library, London, Monty Hammond, Albert Heal, Charles Heal, Jessie Henderson, Historical Records Agency, London, Mary Hobbs, Horrington School, London College of Arms, Les Long, Mendip District Council, Keith Miller, National Market Traders Federation, Councillor Harry Parkes, the Phelps family, Ian Poynter, Priddy School, Public Records Office, London, Jimmy Rawlings and family, John Rosenthal, St Joseph and St Theresa School, St Lawrence School, John Smith and family, Owen Smith, William Smith, Somerset Archaeological and Natural History Society, Somerset County Council, Somerset Records Office, Taunton, Philip Stevens and family, Wells Blue School, Wells Cathedral Administrator John Roberts, Wells Cathedral School, Wells Chamber of Commerce, Wells City Lions, Wells Library, Wells Museum, Wells St John Ambulance, *Western Daily Press*, *Western Gazette*, Peter Wicks, Fred Wilcox and *The World's Fair*.

Very special thanks must go to the following, for putting up with seemingly endless enquiries, all of whom have been so helpful, kind and patient in their response: Keith Donoghue, (Town Clerk for Wells City Council), Alan and Margaret Southwood (doyens of Wells showland knowledge), Ernie Taylor (Bristol area showmen historian), and Michael Chamberlain and Philip Welch (editorial supremos of *The Wells Journal*).

CHAPTER 1

Beginnings

Wells is England's smallest city, situated on the lower slopes of the Mendip Hills on the edge of the Somerset Levels.

Its cathedral is arguably the most beautiful in Europe, enhanced by the magnificent Bishop's Palace, with its wide moated waters, and the Vicar's Close, the oldest intact street in Europe. The city has many other fine old buildings of historical interest, a fit setting for its traditional charter fairs and markets.

During three years, 1998–2001, the people of Wells have enjoyed a unique double celebration: in 1998, the 700th anniversary of the Market Place charter fairs and markets and in 2001 the 800th anniversary of the signing of the first royal charter.

Though that first royal charter was granted by King John in 1201, the history of the Wells charters goes back still further in time. It was under King Ine, ruler of the West Saxons, that the original cathedral was built. Dedicated to St Andrew, it was the very first minster church of the city, built at the time that St Adhelm was consecrated the first Bishop of Sherborne in AD 705. In AD 766, King Cynewulf granted land to the minster church, which was known as the 'Great Spring', later the 'Wells', eventually becoming the name of the township.

The very first grant of fairs and markets was approved by Bishop Robert, during his period of office from 1136 to 1174. The Minster church was to begin a long period of reconstruction to become Wells Cathedral. Perhaps more important still for the people of Wells, in 1160 Robert granted weekly markets and three fairs under the city's first charter. Typical of all similar events in England at the time, these markets and fairs were held inside the Minster itself.

The three charter fairs were to be held on:

May 3rd	Invention of the Holy Cross
October 14th	St Calixtus
November 30th	St Andrew

Bishop Robert's charter included the precautionary requirement:

Charter granted to Wells by King John, September 7, 1201. [Wells City Council]

10

> Whereas the noise and disorder of Markets held in the Church and vestibule of the Church being dishonour to God, disturbance to the ministering Priests and hindrance to the worshippers; lest the Church should become a den of merchandise, henceforth, the Markets on three days of the year . . . shall be no longer held near the Church, but in the broad places of the town.

Between 1174 and 1180, Bishop Reginald, the fourth Bishop of Bath, reaffirmed the charter granted by Robert, allowing Wells borough status, following with a further charter:

> Charter of inspection by Bishop Reginald, Bishop of Bath, of a Charter of Robert, Bishop of Bath, ordaining that those who come to Wells for business on the three festivals . . . shall conduct their business in the places of that will, and shall not presume to violate the Church or the Church porch.

With this charter, Reginald added a fourth fair, on the Anniversary of the Dedication of St Thomas the Martyr, with the days and their 'vigils', adding that the traders would not be subject to tolls. In a later charter, Bishop Savaric reaffirmed that the four charter fairs should be held in the streets instead of on church grounds, with each fair lasting three days.

On September 7th, 1201 the people of Wells were granted their first royal charter. It was signed by King John in Chinon in France, and given to Simon, the Archdeacon of Wells, granting and confirming that Wells might be a free borough, and that the men of the same and their heirs be free burgesses, and that there might be a weekly market on Sundays and free fairs once a year on the Feasts of the Invention of the Holy Cross, St Calixtus, St Andrew, the Morrow of St Andrew and, in addition, the King's gift of a fair on the Feast of the Translation of St Andrew to last for eight days.

For one hundred years, from around 1220, Wells was to enjoy its greatest period of prosperity, with the town then being the fourth largest in the country.

The first known record of Wells High Street is documented in 1228, with today's High Street being known originally as Cheap Street by virtue of the market stalls lining the length of its centre. At the south west of the High Street, Bishop Jocelyn and his brother Hugh, the Archdeacon, founded the Hospital of St John around 1230, under the control of a prior. The Priory served the needs of travellers and wayfarers, offering rest and lodging, as well as help for those who fell ill on their travels.

King Henry III granted Wells its second royal charter on July 14th, 1231.

William Smith, the City of Wells archivist, in his excellent paper 'Trading in medieval Wells', records:

. . . trading was conducted in the High Street, known as Cheap Street (Chepestret) from the Anglo-Saxon 'ceap', meaning market. This accords with the provisions of the early charters, which permitted trading in 'placeis ville' or in 'placeis burgi', in the open spaces of the town or borough. In classical Latin 'platea' usually meant street, as it often did in late Latin, when it is frequently spelt 'placea', having a transferred meaning of a wide open space, such as, though not always, a 'market place', but also the Spanish plaza and Italian piazza, as well as a street. Trading in 'placeis' free of toll or charge on certain specified days was allowed by the Bishops in whose 'dominium' the medieval borough lay.

In 1286, a charter for all charter fairs and markets came into operation, known as 'Pie Powder Courts' or the 'Pieds Poudreux'. 'Dusty Feet' was an appropriate description, given the nature of trading in those days. The laws and regulations concerning charter fairs and markets were strict, with a tight control of price and quality of goods changing hands.

The ceremonial might include the reading of the charter's proclamation or 'crying of the fair', often a long exercise, carried out by the Beadle, the Town Clerk or the Town Crier. Backing this up would be a Court of Justice for each day of the fair.

The fairs and markets in those days were lively, colourful affairs, with live-stock and commodities changing hands, amusements, even public hangings, all held on Saints' Days. The atmosphere of the fairs ranged from the bawdy, to the boisterous and barbaric; yet they were part of a vital, integral network of such trading centres that spread to other fairs on the 'trading routes' to London, like Weyhill in Hampshire, Whitedown in Somerset and Woodbury in Dorset – part and parcel of the Tin Way from Cornwall and the Gold Way from Wales, culminating in London, with cattle going to Smithfield's Bartholomew Fair and horses to Barnet and Horncastle.

The livestock changing hands at these markets, as to be expected, were cattle, sheep and geese, along with horses and ponies. The commodity trading in the Middle Ages saw much dealing in wool and grain from English merchants, while the Continentals, mainly the French, would bring 'exotic' goods such as silks and cottons, along with precious metals.

For entertainment, the early fairground attractions included booths featuring travelling players, puppets and marionettes, along with peep shows. Outside, minstrels, jugglers, acrobats and fire-eaters would perform. Early games of chance, for prizes such as combs, scissors, thimbles, spoons, knives and rings, were precursors of today's modern fairground events.

Minstrels would sing, dancing girls perform, cheapjacks offer cures for warts, toothache and the plague, and pick-pockets would be busy slipping in and out of the crowds. Prostitutes plied their trade, taking their clients back to the appropriately named Grope Lane, today's Union Street.

All this mayhem, mirrored throughout the country, caused distress to many and in 1298, under pressure from the Church, King Edward I would sign an Act of Parliament decreeing that all fairs and markets should be held in the streets and away from church property.

CHAPTER 2

'A Neat Clean City'

Edward's first Act of Parliament caused much debate, for there was great pride in holding fairs and markets inside the churches and cathedrals of the land, and arguments for and against would reverberate for many years to come.

At the peak of its prosperity, Wells was to see the establishment of several trade guilds: the Butchers, including glovers and tanners; the Cordwainers, including ropemakers and tailors; the Hammerers, including metal workers and smiths; the Mercers, including brewers and inn-keepers; the Tuckers, including fullers; the Weavers, including barbers and the Woolcombers, including stocking makers. Cheese-making, especially that of farmhouse Cheddar, was also a thriving industry in the area.

Inflation has made price comparisons virtually meaningless, but it is still interesting to see how much livestock and food cost in those days. A cow might be bought for 12/6d (62p); a pig for 3/6d (17p); a horse for 13/6d (67p), and a sheep for just ½d (6p). Ale cost a penny a gallon (1p for four litres) while a dozen eggs cost just one penny. By comparison a bible (hand-written, and taking five years to complete) could cost a staggering £30.

To put these prices in perspective, a labourer earned little more than one penny a day, perhaps rising at harvest time to two pence – a reminder that those early charter fairs might also serve as 'hiring' fairs where men would go looking for work. After the 'Black Death' of 1348 and 1349, there was a widespread shortage of agricultural workers and King Edward III brought in legislation for able-bodied men and women to make themselves available at the charter fairs. Labourers seeking work would wear an emblem of their trade: a shepherd would have a tuft of wool, a thatcher strands of straw, and for the 'mop' term, maids would come to the fairs carrying their mops and brooms.

The prosperity of Wells declined somewhat, and the looming plague added to the townsfolk's problems. It's long been believed, without official records to confirm it, that during the plague years the fairs and markets were moved out of the confined streets, to be located at Mendip hillside villages such as Binegar and Priddy. Intriguingly, all that remains of those troubled times is the ever popular Priddy Sheep Fair which eventually came to be held in August each year.

Standing beside a now symbolic stack of wooden hurdles, used as enclosures for groups of sheep, a weathered sign reads:

> These hurdles are a symbolic reconstruction of the original collection which were stored here to form pens for the Sheep Fair, which moved from Wells to Priddy in 1348 at the outbreak of the Black Death. . . . The Fair is now held annually on the nearest Wednesday to the original date of the 21st of August.

What the sign does not say is that, with the calendar change of 1752, the Fair was originally staged on the 10th of the month, St Lawrence's Day, but whether this was the actual date in 1348 is open to question, as for a period the Priddy Fair was also held in October!

One Priddy Fair myth is that, should it rain on Fair Day or soon after, that day would then be the first day of winter. Likewise, if the ancient stack of hurdles should ever be removed from the Lower Green, that would signal the end of Priddy Fair.

Around this time, tolls charges were, for a horse and cart load, one penny; a horse load, half a penny and for a man's load, one farthing. On top of these charges, stall hire for traders cost 12d (5p) a day, and there is an example of a farmer's wife, selling eggs and farm produce, having to pay 2d (1p) a day; this sum might amount to a week's rent for a good small-holding, while a serving man might earn up to £2 a year.

The charter fairs at Bridgwater and Wells were the two most notable in the West Country, mixing country and town, with sheep and cattle being bought and sold, along with cloth and flax, and butter and cheese among the principal commodities.

In September, 1451, a letter patent was approved by Thomas Beckington, Bishop of Bath and Wells, for the building of his water conduit in the Market Place. After the ravages and destruction of the Black Death, Bishop Beckington would be responsible for a cleaner and improved city of Wells. His major 'new works' begun in 1451 was for a long terrace of 12 buildings on the north side of the Market Place, which now serve as shops and offices. At the north-east corner is the Penniless Porch, which on the cathedral side, above the archway, displays the bishop's crest.

In the aftermath of the Black Death, in the period 1504–1518, Wells was to enter its lowest period, in terms of trade and prosperity. The textile trade, which had been the core business, was hit by a general slump. Charter fairs and markets survived these bleak times, coming under fire from King Henry VIII during the dissolution of the monasteries, but lost only a few of their rights.

In 1520, the appearance of the Market Place changed, with the construction of the Market and Assize Hall built in the central area, while a High Cross was built on what is today's raised area of the 'Enhancement'. On May 17th, 1554, Queen Mary signed the 20th Royal Charter for Wells.

During the sixteenth century, after struggling through the severe decline in trade, the city's fortunes began to improve, with a revival of the textile industry, with farmhouse cheddar cheese growing in popularity, and now a major commodity at the charter fairs and markets. In the nearby Mendip Hills, the lead mines were becoming more profitable.

Records show that in 1571, the market stalls in the middle of the High Street, in a long building known as the Shambles, prospered, with trade in meat and fish being especially lucrative.

The Market Place was a popular spot for people to congregate, with the Conduit as a focal point. Preachers would often use such focal points, especially on fair and market days, when local streets and roads were closed off. Anyone wanting access, with or without carts or wagons, would have to pay a toll. Local hostelries, too, were good places to do business.

Charter fairs of the 1600s and 1700s were still carried out under canvas, but the occasional hand-made roundabout made its appearance, moved by horse and cart. Separate areas were set aside for selling cattle, horses, pigs and sheep, along with farm produce; while the wares on offer became increasingly diverse, with leather goods, crockery, harnesses and rope.

Consumer protection was not unknown in these early days, and much harsher than it is today. Bakers who sold substandard bread might be flogged in the street, while there are cases of butchers and fishmongers being put in the local stocks, while their condemned produce was burned beneath their noses! Anyone found stealing was severely punished by death, and pillories, whipping posts, stocks and gallows were a sinister feature of life in the market place.

Even the Market Cross and the nearby fountains and water troughs were put to use; water might be brought to boiling point before the victim was scalded to death. It was not unknown for women to be burnt at the stake for murder or witchcraft.

It is not recorded whether such events happened in Wells' Market Place, but the Keward Meadows, to the south-west of the city, were infamous killing fields, with burnings alive and hangings known to have taken place there.

But gradually the importance of the open-air markets declined as more business was conducted in the growing number of coaching inns. These inns often had their seedy side, being frequented by ladies of ill repute; but the Red Lion, on the edge of the Market Place at the top of the High Street, was to become a temperance house in 1600.

By 1640, the population of Wells had grown to around 2,000. The markets, as elsewhere in the country, were still very unhygienic places. During the 1665 Plague, fearful traders would insist on customers putting the correct amount of

Beckington's original conduit in Wells Market Place, 1700s.
[Somerset Archaeological & Natural History Society]

money in jars of vinegar, and would often chew on tobacco hoping to ward off germs. Tar barrels were burned to help clean the air.

It is a pity television had not been invented in those days, for these old markets were very colourful places: an incredible mêlée of traders, ordinary folk, pick-pockets, prostitutes, all talking and shouting, bells ringing, dogs barking, cows bellowing, sheep bleating and pigs grunting – all this mayhem adding up to a bewildering, exciting, yet strangely beautiful pageant of life. No wonder that later writers like Charles Dickens and Thomas Hardy found them a wealth of inspiration.

Generally, the streets remained little more than insanitary cess-pits, but things were changing slowly, with Bishop Beckington's gift of water to the city flowing from the conduit on either side of the city's streets, giving the opportunity to clean the central area.

The year 1685 saw the Market Hall in the Market Place, also known as the Exchequer, become the venue for the visit of Lord Chief Judge George Jeffreys. The Exchequer was the setting of his seventh and last round of the notorious 'Bloody Assizes', set up after the Monmouth Rebellion in the Battle of Sedgemoor, 15 miles to the south-west of Wells.

Of 696 prisoners, 543 were tried and 383 known to have been sentenced to transportation and eight poor souls were hung, drawn and quartered before being boiled, salted and finally tarred.

Ten years later, the Quaker William Penn (later to be known for founding Pennsylvania in North America) preached to a crowd of 2,000 people from an upstairs window of the Crown Hotel, overlooking the Market Place.

In the 500 years from 1174 to 1694, no fewer than 34 charters and letters patent were approved, 30 being royal grants. Few cities and towns can match this record.

The dawn of the eighteenth century saw the coming of the factory and mill, which would change the face of the English countryside for ever. In Wells, the industrial areas grew up in the south and west of the city, with the Market Place, Cathedral and Bishop's Palace remaining a haven of tranquillity. The noted writer Daniel Defoe visited Wells and in *A Tour Through the Whole Island of Great Britain*, published yearly from 1724 to 1726, he described the cathedral as 'the most beautiful in the island', and Wells itself as 'a neat clean city', with 'no want of good company there'.

Another commentator, writing in the *Book of Fairs* in 1729, said 180 charter fairs were now being held in Somerset alone, with Bridgwater and Wells still the 'most respected of them all'. In 1734, William Sever, writing in *Wells*, dealt in depth with the 1589 royal charter granted by Elizabeth, while a year later, a plan of Wells was engraved by William Simes, delineating the Market Place, with its High Cross, the central Market Hall and Bishop Thomas Beckington's 'New Works'.

The market stalls in the centre of the High Street were to be removed in 1754 and relocated for a period in a yard behind the then rebuilt Queen's Arms, while a part of the Shambles, known also as Middle Row, was dismantled.

In the same year, worried by the increased number of beggars, the Corporation approved of the role of a beadle to drive them out of town.

Out on the Mendip hillside village of Binegar, according to the Reverend J. Collinson writing in 1792 in *The History and Antiquities of the County of Somerset*, Binegar Fair was 'a very large fair, lasting the whole Whitsun Week', and 'anciently held in the High Street of Wells'. This fair is believed to have been another of Wells' five main charter fairs, most likely one of its two May Fairs, 'the Invention of the Holy Cross' or 'The Transition of St Andrew', with Bishop Charles Moss in 1792 demanding a fee of 10 shillings for its return to the streets of Wells.

An Act of Parliament in 1779, signed by George III, allowing charter fairs and markets in the Market Place, took them out of the control of the bishops and into that of the corporation. A new Town Hall was to be built, replacing the Canonical House owned by the Bishop, and which would give the Market Place its unique, inverted L-shaped area.

CHAPTER 3

'Innocent Amusements of the Poorer Classes'

In most English cities, the town hall, of whatever size or splendour, is usual situated in a prominent, eye-catching location. Wells Town Hall is different. The visitor entering in a north-easterly direction along the High Street, will look in vain, for it is tucked away to the south of the inverted L-shaped Market Place. One reason for this apparent reticence is the towering cathedral, looking down over the rooftops of Bishop Beckington's 'New Works'. If the Town Hall had been constructed on this northern side, the cathedral would have been obscured.

In contrast, if one approaches the Market Place walking south westerly, through the Penniless Porch archway, the view of the town hall is stunning, making a perfect complement to the Market Place.

Into the nineteenth century, the Market Place was now becoming very popular as an 'open cheese market', while the charter fairs of May and October were more popular for livestock.

In 1796, a Gothic-style conduit was constructed in the Market Place to replace Bishop Beckington's conduit which had now fallen into disrepair. In the same year, Wells saw probably its first travelling circus, presented by the Fossett family. There were no wild or exotic animals, and the show people, having only horses and ponies, showed off their equestrian skills on the Cathedral Green.

By 1801, the first Census showed the Wells population to be around 2,500 people. The charter fairs were dwindling, and the once free trading had all but gone, with dealers, sellers and traders having to pay their 'stallage' or 'pickage'.

If the Fossetts had been the first circus people to visit Wells, the Miles family are widely believed to be the first to bring a travelling menagerie. The 'Miles Family Collection of Living Curiosities' is recorded in 1809. They brought exotic creatures never before seen in the area – lions, tigers, leopards, kangaroos and ostriches, along with eagles, falcons and vultures. In 1813, the Ballard Family Menagerie and Waxworks Show similarly pulled in huge crowds.

In the mid-1830s, the Wells Turnpike Trusts were improving transport links, upgrading the main approaches to the city. Inns and hostelries prospered, with

The Market Place in the 1800s: lithograph by George Rowe.
[Somerset Archaeological & Natural History Society]

horse-drawn coaches and mail coaches now approaching their swansong era. At this time, the showmen and their families were changing from tented accommodation to mobile homes, 'living trailers' and 'living wagons'.

In 1836, a new Market Hall was built in the Market Place at a cost of £3,269, with the building soon to take over the running of the former open cheese market. In 1839, the Market Place was enlarged once more, and in the same year the railway age reached Wells, when it was linked to nearby Glastonbury by the Somerset Central Railway.

By mid-century, the population of Wells had grown further. There was a decline in the textile trade, but at Haybridge on the outskirts of the city, the St Cuthbert's Mill opened in 1850, specialising in paper manufacture.

The Industrial Revolution brought with it the era of steam, and Charles Heal and Sons, originating from nearby Glastonbury, were to become one of the most respected show-land families and central to the success of the twice-yearly Wells Charter Fairs. During the fairs, the streets would glow with the warmth and colour of the naphtha lamps, while huge organs played inside the growing number of hand-carved and decorated 'scenic' riding machines.

The Fair Acts of 1871 and 1873 caused much confusion between charter and non-charter fairs, leading the Home Secretary, Sir William Vernon-Harcourt to instruct the police that no attempt should be made to interfere with 'the innocent amusements of the poorer classes'. In 1890, the Secretary of State ruled that nearby Glastonbury's Tor Fair should take place on the second Monday of September and last for eight days.

The Victorian era saw the advent of three railways to Wells. But the city has maintained its twin roles of cathedral city and market town, and its limited scope for trade and industry has probably been its salvation, retaining its medieval structure. Many long established family firms are still in business, with many 150 years old. The names of the showmen were by now being documented, with the Moores Brothers' boxing booth a great favourite in the 1890s.

The brothers' boxing booth was known as 'Professor Moore's National Sporting Pavilion', though to Wellensians it quickly became known as Bill Moore's Boxing Booth. William Moore had his daughters sparring in the ring, but only against each other, or with their brother, Albert – even, occasionally, with a bear!

A smallpox outbreak in 1896 curtailed the scope of the May Charter Fair, with just a few side stalls. In 1897, the Phillips family took what is believed to be the earliest photograph of this fair, showing a bustling Market Place full with attractions. The present Charles Heal reckons some of his forbears are probably pictured in the photograph. The Rawlings and Smith families have been setting up for business outside the Crown Inn for over a hundred years, a right granted, according to Jimmy Rawlings, by King John!

A classic image of the Wells May Fair, 1897. [Alan Southwood]

The first named attraction in the Market Place is that of the Pruett family's 'Four Abreast Gallopers', appearing in 1900 at the May Charter Fair and the St Andrews Fair in December. The Pruetts were Bristol-based showmen, established about 1891. They also travelled a small 'Cinematograph Show', but after their visits of 1903, a family dispute led to the set of 'Gallopers' and their traction engine 'Pride of Bristol' being laid up in a field to slowly rot away until 1934, when they were set alight on Bonfire Night.

1904 saw a visit by the renowned Colonel W.F. Cody, one of America's greatest showmen. Better known as Buffalo Bill, his entourage arrived in three special trains, complete with 500 horses and a staff of 800, including 100 North American Indians.

Meanwhile the gap left by the Pruetts was filled by the Hancock and Cole families, with their 'switchback' and other attractions. In the 1908 May Charter Fair, Charles Heal & Sons made their first appearance in their own right, with their own set of 'Four Abreast Gallopers', and the attraction of an 89-key Marenghi organ. This year saw the last December St Andrew's Fair. Six years earlier, the November Wells Carnival had commenced, and was proving immensely popular, and it was agreed that from 1909 the two events should take place together, being then held on Tuesdays and Wednesdays.

Britain's answer to Buffalo Bill was the showmen, Bostock and Wombwell's 'Royal No. 1 Menagerie', visiting the Market Place in 1909, while the carnival prizes were awarded on the stage of Anderton and Rowland's 'Theatre of Varieties Show' in the same year. In 1910, the awards were presented on the stage of W.C. and S. Hancock's 'Living Picture Show'.

Charter fairs and markets were changing, and the likes of Weyhill in Hampshire and the much fabled Whitedown Fair in Somerset were becoming part of the folklore of 'Old England'. Wells, meanwhile, was hanging on to its monthly livestock markets, conducted by auctioneers such as Bennet, Millard and Lloyd, Bowring and W.H. Palmer, H.C. and W.E. Budd, Collins and Son, Laver and Son and Moody and Son. Of all the monthly auctions, the May Fair Market still pulled the biggest crowds.

From 1908, Charles Heal and Sons continued to hold court in the Market Place, with the staging of the twice-yearly charter fairs, though other unofficial fairs were also being held around the city, such as in Webb's Field in Priory Road, today the site of Homechime.

The First World War was to take the lives of 99 Wellensians. To keep the charter intact, a few stalls were erected in Market Place in 1919. In 1915, the *Wells Journal* was reporting of the May Charter Fair that 'this old time festival suffered from the effects of the war; it was but a skeleton of its former splendour'.

Charles Heal, unable to return to the Market Place in 1919, staged their own 'unofficial' May Fair on the Webb's Field site, helping to keep rival

Early photograph of Charles Heal and family. [Ernie Taylor]

Charles Heal's famous living wagon, now in collection of Bristol Industrial Museum. [Ernie Taylor]

Charles and Agnes Heal and children. [Ernie Taylor]

Glastonbury Tor Fair, 1907: the early home town fair of Charles Heal. [Ernie Taylor]

The Pruett family rides seen in 1934, after being abandoned after a family dispute. They last came to Wells in 1903. [Ernie Taylor]

Inside the Venetian Gondolas, standing alongside the organ is Percy Cole, whose family presented many Wells 'Confetti Fairs'. [Ernie Taylor]

Charles Heal's 89-key Marenghi Organ, out of the Four Abreast Gallopers. Charles (on the left) is seen with Alf Smith.
[Ernie Taylor]

The young boy sitting on the steps of the Cole family's Venetian Gondolas shows the size of the Victorian riding machines. [Ernie Taylor]

31

showmen away. The *Journal* reported that 'unusually large crowds were in attendance'.

1920, though, was to see a feast of travelling showmen, starting with Ernest Hill presenting his 'Four Abreast Gallopers' and supporting amusements on the Webb's Field location at the end of April of that year. Charles Heal, meanwhile, was back in the Market Place on Friday April 30th and the following day, while on the Cathedral Green on Saturday a special May Fair featured a 'Cake Walk' among its rides, billed as 'the Wiggle Woggle from Coney Island' and a helter-skelter. In this year, Charles Heal and Sons and fellow-showmen started a 'Benefit Night' for the Wells and District Cottage Hospital.

'The Market Place is the natural home of the Fair,' was the welcoming comment of the *Wells Journal*. So popular were Charles Heal and his fellow travellers that they opened up for business the following Saturday on Webb's Field. At Sam McKeowan's Boxing Booth, Wells police-sergeant Cross had a match with Bert Rolls, while Bill Langdon from Street had a 10-round contest. It was here also that the first recorded accident at the fair took place, when a person fell from one of the rides and was sent to the nearby Workhouse Infirmary.

If this was not outdoor pleasure enough, on Friday May 14th the Market Place saw the return of Bostock and Wombwell with their 'Great United Show'.

By the late 1920s, Charles Heal and Sons were really pulling in the crowds, and continuing with the benefit nights for the local hospital. Extra late-night trains had to be laid on, while over 5,000 people used the late-night special buses.

'Around this revolving galaxy of colouring were the usual odd assortment of allurements which contribute to the undeniable fascination of an English Fair,' wrote the local newspaper of the 1921 May event, while 'The 1925 Wells May Fair should go down to history as a veritable triumph for soap and water!'

The 1930s saw the Depression, and in Wells the Penniless Porch became known as the 'Beggars Eye', so many people were converging there. After the 1931 May Charter Fair, on Wednesday May 6th, Bostock and Wombwell paid their final visit to the city, as part of their farewell tour, setting up in the Market Street livestock area. In the following year, Dorothy Shilton and Richard Holworthy published *Wells City Charters*, detailing the actual documents.

'Wells May Fair not losing its appeal to country folk' in the *Wells Journal* made for happy reading:

> Any idea prevailing that Wells May Fair is losing its annual appeal to citizens and rural dwellers was strongly rebutted on Saturday last, when from an early hour country folk flocked into Wells to attend this ancient Spring Festival.
> In accordance with long established custom, the Pleasure Fair has pitched in the Market Place; the whole space available had been let to Charles Heal, featuring Gallopers, Noah's Ark and Dodgems, along

Charter Fair Tapestries [All photos: Caroline Bagias]

1200s - St Joseph and St Theresa School, Wells.

1300s - Priddy School.

1400s - Stoberry Park
Junior School, Wells.

1500s - St Lawrence
School, Westbury-sub-
Mendip.

1600s - Primary School,
Chewton Mendip.

1700s - Horrington
School.

1800s - Wells Blue
School.

1900s - Stoberry
Park Infants School,
Wells.

with Shooting Galleries, Freak Shows, Shaded Boudoirs, into which one could surely enter Dame Fortune, and Coconut Shies!

A feature of the Fair was the excellent order maintained by the large crowd, the event passing off in a most orderly fashion, there being very few incidents necessitating police intervention.

In 1935, the story was slightly different, with the newspaper reporting, 'There were no galloping horses, which seemed to have gone the way their living counterparts are going, and have been ousted by mechanised steeds.'

If Charles Heal and Sons were doing good business with the May event, for a period in the 1930s it was the Cole family who were in charge at the November Carnival Charter Fair, with a regular 'Confetti Battle' as part of the billed 'Old Country Fair'. From 1930 to 1935, this unique event would see over 1,000 bags of confetti used. From 1936 to 1938, Anderton and Rowland took over the winter presentation, while the Heal family remained in control of the summer event.

Another book on the local fairs was published in 1936. Writing in *A Historical Survey of Somerset Fairs*, the Reverend N.F. Hulbert reported that by 1933 the number of charter fairs and markets in the county had declined to just over 30.

The last May Fair before the Second World War, in 1939, was to be very special, with Charles Heal asking for an extra day to help build up the firm's newest ride, the 'Moon Rocket', a huge attraction that was to be part of its later downfall, but was the 'white knuckle' ride of the era.

The *Journal* was in nostalgic mood: 'The Chocolate Kings were on their usual stand, but where were the Fish and Chip Saloons? One missed a certain aroma, when passing their pitch.'

Complementing the Moon Rocket were the Heals' Dodgems and Noah's Ark, making what was to be the last full-size Market Place Charter Fair until the November Carnival of 1946.

Regarding the May Cattle Market and Show, the newspaper reported that 'at least one piebald horse was brought to the Fair for luck', and commenting on the Charter Fair itself, 'The Fair continued until past midnight, when the square still contained a large crowd; by mid-day Sunday, the Market Place was spick and span again, and one hardly realised that such a transformation could take place in so few hours.'

To uphold the charters, the showmen would present only a handful of stalls during the Second World War, for they had to do their bit for the country, often leaving the wives to 'keep the show on the road'. Fairs in general were to become very thin on the ground, though for Wells, in September 1941, Henry Rogers presented his Ark, along with Joe Heal's juvenile ride and supporting attractions, at the Home Field of the Palace Farm. In 1943, the same venue saw

John Gratton's coconut shy was a regular attraction at the Wells charter fairs. [Ernie Taylor]

Charles Heal with the Embling Brothers (The Chocolate Kings) at a 1930's Wells May Fair.
[Alan Southwood]

Several of the Heal family's rides were destroyed in the Bristol blitz. [Ernie Taylor]

Charles Heal & Sons' Burrell showman's engine 'England's Glory'. [Ernie Taylor]

The Burrell traction engine 'Her Majesty'. [Ernie Taylor]

37

The Burrell traction engine 'His Majesty' in 1937. [Ernie Taylor]

The Burrell 'White Rose of York' in 1937. [Ernie Taylor]

The pulling power of the Heals' engine 'Her Majesty' in action in 1938. [Ernie Taylor]

On the road with 'His Majesty'. [Ernie Taylor]

The pulling power of Albert Heal's Scammell 'Britannia' with some of the Moon Rocket loads. [Ernie Taylor]

Alf Cooper's Boxing Booth stands outside Penniless Porch. [Ernie Taylor]

Albert Heal's Moon Rocket ride fully built up, 1939. [Alan Southwood]

The size of the central construction of the Moon Rocket clearly shows its logistical problems.
[Ernie Taylor]

Wells May Fair in the 1930s, with Charles Heal's Dodgems, Noah's Ark and Gallopers. [Alan Southwood]

Charles Heal's Jungle Speedway at a 1950s Wells May Fair. [Alan Southwood]

two fairs, with the Cole family's 'Venetian Gondolas' and stalls appearing at the end of April and mid-May seeing Anderton and Rowland's Ark and Mrs Lock's Dodgems in attendance.

Mrs Lock's Dodgems were to reappear for the May Fair of 1944, and were this time to be found on the Dairy Field in Glastonbury Road, in attendance with Sam Smart's Four Abreast Gallopers. The *Wells Journal* reported, 'Man power for the War effort affects even Amusement Caterers, and to make up for this, local men were employed as assistants on the amusements, while the women took the money on the galloping horses.'

The Second World War took its toll of the business of Charles Heal and Sons. During one raid in the Bristol Blitz, several rides were blown into matchwood, but by 1945 the Bristol and Glastonbury-based showmen were in Wells for the May Fair, now held on the Recreation Ground. During their stay, the welcome news came through that hostilities had ceased, and the fair stayed on for an extra week to be part of the VE celebrations.

By 1946 the May Cattle Market and Show saw 'the gypsies on the Mermaid corner [who] gave their free display of fisticuffs, stripped to the waist, caused much amusement to the large crowd,' reported the *Journal* as some aspects of normal life began to return to the city.

Sadly, on the way to the Wells May Charter Fair of 1950, Charles Heal, Snr – known affectionately as the 'Great Man' – fell ill, and passed away at the Wells Cottage Hospital, with which his family had, and still have, strong links by virtue of their ever popular benefit nights.

Questions were now being asked about the siting of the Fair, but most people wanted it to remain in the Market Place. 'This ancient charter allowing the use of the Market Place is a privilege, belonging to the citizens which we should be chary of taking away. I don't see why this council should interfere with the privileges granted to the citizens,' was the view of Councillor Kippax, while Alderman Aldcocks added, 'This is a very old established custom, many of which are disappearing in these days.'

Friday, September 7th, 1951 was a day of festivities to mark the 750th anniversary of the signing of the first royal charter, and while the twice-yearly fairs and twice-weekly markets were as popular as ever, the monthly livestock markets were going into decline.

In 1953, the *Journal* reporting on the May Charter Fair lamented that 'There were no ice-cream or fish and chip restaurants on wheels, and again one missed the familiar sight of past days, the cheap jacks and quacks; in fact the Fair was quite respectable!'

Despite this positive coverage, a minority still wanted the twice-yearly event moved out of its long established home. But feelings were mixed. Times were certainly changing, and at the 1956 May Fair, there was to be the first instance of trouble, with 'Teddy Boys' setting on fair employees, Wellensians and country folk coming to their rescue.

1957 saw the last official May Cattle Market Show and Sale, organised by the Wells, Glastonbury and District Young Farmers Club, for the cattle pens were soon to be dismanted by the council and the land turned over to car parking.

THESE HURDLES ARE A SYMBOLIC
RECONSTRUCTION OF THE ORIGINAL
COLLECTION WHICH WERE STORED
HERE TO FORM THE PENS FOR THE
SHEEP FAIR WHICH MOVED FROM
WELLS TO PRIDDY IN 1348 AT THE
OUTBREAK OF THE BLACK DEATH.
THE FAIR IS NOW HELD ANNUALLY
ON THE NEAREST WEDNESDAY TO
THE ORIGINAL DATE OF THE 21ST AU

The sign says it all: taken at the 1995 Priddy Sheep Fair. [Richard Green]

BBC Radio Bristol's Roger Bennett with Alf Cooper at the 1998 Priddy Sheep Fair. The Coopers' Boxing Booth attended the Wells May Fairs in the 1950s. [Richard Green]

The hog roast at the 1998 Priddy Sheep Fair dates back to the mop fair era. [Richard Green]

Two of the original ingredients, amusements and livestock, are still part
of the Priddy Sheep Fair. [Richard Green]

CHAPTER 4

'Ancient Customs should be Preserved'

Having survived the Black Death, two world wars and a major economic depression, the twice-yearly Charter Fairs were again under pressure. It was in 1958 that the first concerted attempts were made to secure their future. The *Wells Journal* led the way, asking the question on its front page: 'Should Market Place Fairs Find Alternative Site?'

'Remove to the Recreation Ground,' say R. Godfrey, of J.N. Knight and Sons, the ironmongers, while Mrs Southwood of Phillips Studio responded, 'I'm opposed to any move.' 'Live and let live,' added Mrs G.E. Wilkins of the Anchor Restaurant.

'I should hate to stop giving pleasure to these people, there are too few of these old customs being kept alive,' opined Ernest Gregory from Gregory's Radio. 'The Heal Family are extremely co-operative,' responded F.R. Brown, a director of Clares, while A. H. Russell, the Head Postmaster, said, 'We are not inconvenienced a great deal by the Fair.'

The *Journal* balanced the business opinion with a survey of newly elected councillors, with the balance of opinion being for no change, with the argument being put forward by the Wells Preservation Society and others that the fairs 'are held as a right, and an emblem of freedom, granted by the charters of the Bishops, later confirmed by several Royal Charters.'

A photograph of the 1959 May Fair, taken by the late Edward Dyer and reproduced on the front page of the *Wells Journal*, shows Wellensians and country folk voting with their feet, for the event was well patronised.

The following year saw the November Carnival and Charter Fair held on Tuesday and Wednesday for the last time before changing to Thursday and Friday.

In 1963 the community spirit was still very apparent, with the press again reporting 'May Fair gaiety in the Market Place; the ancient May Fair is still a popular Festival with the country folk flocking to the merry-making.'

But in 1967, after a 10-year struggle, the Young Farmers Club bowed to the inevitable trend towards permanent livestock markets and finally abandoned the traditional May Cattle Market Show and Sale. A similar decision was made at Shepton Mallet.

In 1972, Wells survived the threat of losing its status under the Local Government Act, retaining not only its mayor, but also the charters of 1399 and 1589 which remained intact along with the other surviving charters.

Up in the Mendip Hills, the village of Priddy still upheld its ancient 'Sheep Fair', with the 1972 presentation seeing the showmen on the Lower Green, presenting a special August Bank Holiday Fair, lasting from Thursday 24th to Monday 28th, with riding machines, Dodgems, a Waltzer and an Ark.

In 1974, Queen Elizabeth signed yet another Royal Charter, formally giving Wells city status.

But times were changing, and the once tight-knit community spirit was beginning to weaken. Around this time, apart from the annual Carnival which attracted crowds of more than 50,000, the only other major crowd-pulling event was the Moat Boat Races, performed on the waters of the Bishop's Palace. With the YMCA closing its doors and the local youth club declining, there was little for local teenagers to participate in, and these races were to reach their peak when included in the popular BBC 'It's a Knockout' television spectacle. Crowds reached saturation point.

Two huge 'Civil War' re-enactments also drew massive crowds, but there was little else by way of outdoor entertainment, other than regular sporting activities.

There were certain tensions in the city, over car-parking charges and the twice-weekly market traders, irate about rent increases, were threatening to blockade the Market Place, while four main shops closed their doors for ever: Crease, Son and Company, International Stores, Liptons and Oakeshotts Ltd., all in the aftermath of the country's 'three-day working week'.

In the Market Place charter fair, Charles Heal and Sons were still holding court, with the May Fair of 1975 seeing Charles Heal's Dodgems supported by Albert Heal's Hurricane Jets and Joe Heal's Twist, which would remain the basic recipe for the next ten years and more.

But the fairs were not without their critics, with the familiar, if inaccurate, accusation that the Fair had outgrown the Market Place, although the reality was that the Fair, which had hardly changed format since the mid-1800s, was itself being squeezed out of its traditional home. The 1979 and 1980 presentations were blighted by accusations, but Alan Southwood, a local trader, was applauded by the *Fairground Mercury* for his efforts to ensure the continuing tradition.

In 1981, Charles Heal and Sons celebrated their centenary, but were looking at their long-term future, as, with the rest of the country, the halcyon era of the travelling fairs had peaked. At the November Carnival Charter Fair in 1984, there was no Heal family ride, for the first time in living memory; instead

Wellensians vote with their feet, filling up the 1959 May Fair after a negative attack; Charles Heal and Sons won a new three-year contract. [Edward Dyer]

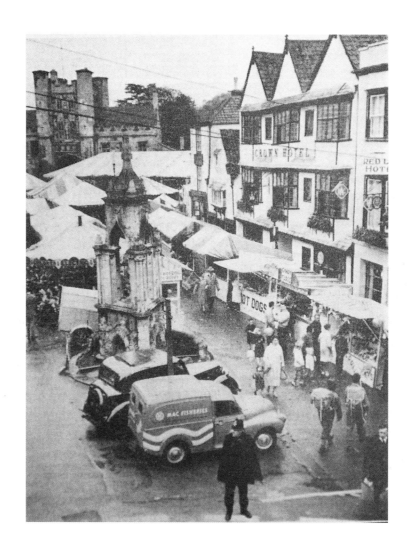

Wells May Fair, 1962, under the auspices of Charles Heal and Sons. [Edward Dyer]

A bird's eye view of the 1965 Carnival Charter Fair. [*Wells Journal*]

Charles Heal and Sons' Big Wheel in May, 1963, as pictured in the *Shepton Mallet, Glastonbury & Axbridge Gazette*. [photo Edward Dyer]

The Rawlings' family classic 'Laughing Clowns' game. [Alan Southwood]

Generations of Rawlings have attended the charter fairs: current regulars, Jimmy and Sonia. [Ernie Taylor]

John Smith Jnr's Cups and Saucers Juvenile Ride. [Richard Green]

One of the last coconut shies to come to Wells was owned by showman John Clements. [Alan Southwood]

May Charter Fair, 1999: loyal tenant Philip Stevens Snr with his Fun House making a colourful focal point.
[Richard Green]

Wiltshire travellers, the Jennings family from Devizes, presented their Dodgems, and the first modern ride of its type, the SuperTrooper, an aerial white-knuckle attraction, while William Rowland presented the more traditional Big Wheel.

Charles Heal's Dodgems made a final appearance at the May Charter Fair in 1986, but although their rides were being sold, and the bulk of their business now based in Brighton, the family firm were still in overall charge of the twice-yearly events.

In May 1987 it was the turn of Amesbury-based showmen Joey Stokes and Sons to make their debut in the Market Place. The next few years were to prove eventful. Among the attractions the Stokes family have owned are Dodgems, Chair-O-Planes, Big Wheel and several sets of Waltzers, along with motive power dating from the showmen's steam traction engine era, including the much fabled John Fowler engine, The Showman. The growing size of the November Carnival crowds caused problems, leading to more rigid police enforcement of the regulations governing the operation of carnival trailers.

In 1988, Joey Stokes and his fellow showmen presented not three but four major rides, with Charles Appleton's Twist, Anderton and Rowland's Meteor, William Whitelegg's (past President of the Showmen's Guild of Great Britain) Invader and Philip Appleton's Rock-O-Plane making a very impressive line-up of attractions – all now compacted into a reduced area and making for a very entertaining evening.

The following year's celebration of the 400th anniversary of the charters of Queen Elizabeth I was somewhat lukewarm, as (like the mid-1970s Charter Weeks) there was no actual fair. The market traders, however, entered into the spirit of the occasion.

1992 saw not only the threat of car parking being removed, but also the twice-yearly Charter Fairs and the twice-weekly markets taken out of the Market Place. Thursday November 12th and Friday the 13th were further fated when the heavens opened to deluge the proceedings.

The Fairs and Markets, now in their 694th year, were about to fight their biggest campaign for survival. Under the heading 'The Final Funfair', the *Wells Journal* reported that 'Wells Fair will never return to the Market Place – despite protests from the fair operator. Just one week after Wells Market stall-holders threatened a pirate action to return to the Market Place, the fun fair operator has now threatened to move onto the city streets if banished from the Market Place – as the square's enhancement scheme working group has ruled it should.'

Showman Joey Stokes replied angrily: 'We have a Charter for the Fair in the streets of Wells. We will go onto those streets if they chuck us out of the Market Place. The Fair has been there for hundreds of years. It is the perfect setting for it and part of Wells' heritage . . . Mendip has not told us we can't come back. The Fair could cope with the raised pavement planned for the Market Place.'

Graham Jeffs, then Chief Executive for Mendip District Council, responded: 'The enhanced Market Place will not be a suitable place to hold a modern fair. Times are changing. The Fair physically can't go there. If we have spent a large sum of money improving the surface, it may be unacceptable for it to go back in case it damages it. . . . The Market Place is the traditional site for a traditional Fair. The modern Fair is quite different because of the methods of entertainment, size of machinery and generators which produce oil drips.'

Showman Michael De-Vey said, 'Carnival night wouldn't be the same without the Fair, and the fairground income would drop by over half if it moved out.'

A few weeks later, the *Journal* was reporting that the Funfair might return after all, quoting Graham Jeffs as saying that a final decision had not yet been taken. The newspaper conducted a straw poll among the locals, with a majority of 9–1 wanting to keep the twice-yearly Charter Fair in the Market Place. One couple summed up the mood: 'We've seen the Fair and Market there for 76 years and in no way would we like to see it go.'

There next followed questions over the legal position, with William Smith, the City Archivist questioning what right the funfair had to stay in the Market Place and, similarly, whether it was legal to move the market temporarily. 'Both issues are contestable in law and only a court could give a definitive ruling.' Different experts interpreted the position differently, and many people saw their livelihoods threatened; not only the showmen, but Market Place shopkeepers worried about the loss of customers' car parking – all this, against the background of national recession.

While all this was going on, Joey Stokes and a group of other showmen tried their luck overseas, taking their rides and attractions to Hong Kong. But the battle of Wells continued, with consultations with the Wells MP, David Heathcoat-Amory and letters to Her Royal Highness, Queen Elizabeth.

In February 1993 the beleaguered market traders faced their worst crisis since the proposed blockade of the Market Place in 1975, with the *Western Gazette* carrying an article 'Traders Face a Shutout', while in March there seemed to be a glimmer of hope when the *Wells Journal* announced 'Market Place Fair Hopes'. The then Father of Wells City Council, Councillor Harry Parkes was one of the few fighting 'the cause', and in a letter pledged: 'I shall continue to do what I can as a City Councillor to support the interests of the Fairs and Market Operators, and the Market Place traders.'

A meeting on March 9th, 1993 between Mendip District Council and representatives of the Showmen's Guild of Great Britain clarified (in summary) the position of the showmen:

> The Fair Operators wish to remain in the Market Place and will go to litigation to defend their Charter Rights.

The May Charter Fair, 1986 saw the very last visit of Charles Heal and Sons' Dodgems. [Richard Green]

Joey Stokes' Trabant, the 'Satellite', lands in the Market Place for the 1993 May Fair.
[Richard Green]

63

'Build up' time at the May Charter Fair, 2000, with showman Billy Cole by the centre of his Waltzer ride, while Charles Heal marks out the allotted 'grounds'. [Richard Green]

A modern-day favourite of the teenagers is the Miami Ride, and at Wells Charles Appleton's Hi-Energy has become a regular visitor. [Richard Green]

Members of the Sealed Knot Society add their period of history to the Wells May Fair. [Alan Southwood]

Only if they failed in law would they contemplate an alternative location.

They would be prepared to operate on a reduced basis if 'Phase 2' construction fell on Fair dates.

The Operators have had experience of working in newly paved areas and feel that they have caused no damage there.

They are prepared to guarantee that any damage would be made good.

Divisions over the future of the Market Place under the Enhancement Scheme were not eased, and at yet another meeting at Wells Town Hall many business-men and women became totally exasperated, often to the point of tears, at the lack of common sense and compassion.

CHAPTER 5

'Celebration or Commemoration'

The first phase of the Market Place enhancement was completed on time. The scheme included the planting of three young trees in the Market Place, which some feared would obstruct the Dodgem track as well as possibly taking away some market stall space.

On a crisp fine blue-skied morning on Thursday April 29th, 1993, lined up in the Chamberlain Street car park, close to the main entrance, were the fleet of Joey Stokes and Sons vehicles; amassed for the 'Pull On', featuring the ERF power unit, 'Simply the Best', with the Dodgem cars box truck and pay box, the Foden 'Spirit of the South' with the trailer mounted 'Satellite' ride and the Foden 'Lady Rachel' with the Dodgem floor and nets, while behind was Joseph Stokes' ERF, with the Waltzer loads.

As with all fair 'pull ons', this was a military operation, conforming to local authority rules, Showmen's Guild procedures and Health and Safety Executive guidance on safe practice for Fairs.

Soon after the local church bells had rung at 8 o'clock, the showmen were back in the new-look Market Place and ready to build the Dodgem track on the new, raised area of the 'First Phase' enhancement.

Within a couple of hours, most of the Dodgem track was in place, and all seemed to be going well when suddenly a television crew arrived, with consent to film in the Market Place on the very same morning! Happily, with give and take on both sides, both events went ahead successfully. The *Journal* commented that 'there was just room for the games and the Fair proprietor Joey Stokes was prepared to wait a while before erecting the two main rides on 'Phase Two'.

This sums up what a working Market Place should be: full of hustle and bustle, a testament to real tradition and a living heritage rather than static preservation. Writing in the *World's Fair* newspaper, Ernie Taylor commented:

> Following a winter of uncertainty, for much of which the lessee (Joey Stokes) was in Hong Kong, the Fair adapted very well to the changes imposed by the restructuring of the Market Place.
> Many people, myself included, think the changes, as far as the Fair is

concerned are an improvement. I made a point of speaking to local people, not specifically interested in the Fair, and found without exception the new arrangements were an improvement. Apparently, the city is divided on the merits of the restructuring, but at least the Fair seems to have surmounted its first perceived obstacle.

Allowing the May Charter Fair to take place and showing that no damage was done, was crucial to the future celebrations: the 700th anniversary of the Wells Market Place Charter Fairs and Markets in 1998, followed by the 800th anniversary of the signing of the first Royal Charter in 2001.

In June 1993, the 620th Mayor of the City of Wells, Councillor Kate Fry, agreed to revive the long overdue 'opening ceremony', to recommence with the forthcoming November Carnival Charter Fair.

With the enhanced Market Place getting so much media attention, other positive projects were proposed for the historic area, including plans for an outdoor café, giving the Market Place a Continental flavour similar to that of the city's two twin towns, Bad Durkheim in Germany and Paray Le Monial in France.

In agreeing to the summer style of an open air café, local councillors deemed that 15 days a year should be set aside for other events, including the May and November Charter Fairs.

Market traders suffered during building works for Phase Two, finding their relocated area somewhat barren and open to the elements. The return to the warmth of the closeted Market Place would have to wait a little longer.

Sadly, many characters of the markets had now gone, notably Jack Davis, a legend in his own lifetime, a much loved man who was not only the Market Toll Collector but Town Crier as well, among many duties. Other characters to have frequented the markets were George and Sylvia Mooney with their china stall. The diminutive George was one of the last of the all-round showmen, having worked in the golden era of the music- and variety-halls as part of an acrobatic troupe. Being the smallest, he usually ended up on top of these feats of human strength!

Probably the longest-serving market trader was Jean Gray, with her cloths and textiles, adding warmth and colour to the stalls, and later a key person behind the scenes, with the 700th Anniversary Charter Fair Tapestry. Other long-standing traders include the Wheddons, who came from nearby Castle Cary, with their fruit and vegetable stall, and Ken Ganfield, who has been coming for more than 15 years.

Later to support the Market Traders on the City Council's Market Place Management Committee and also to be Chairman of Wells Chamber of Commerce is Cheryl Carter who can be found selling her leather goods, alongside husband Richard, who specialises in photograph and picture frames.

Smiles at a sunny Saturday market. [Richard Green]

Wells Saturday Market, 2000, looking towards the Town Hall; the photograph shows details of the enhancement scheme. [Richard Green]

The unique memorial in the Market Place to former Wells Olympic athlete, Mary Bignal-Rand and her then world-breaking long jump at the Tokyo Olympic Games. [Richard Green]; and Bishop Bekynton's row of terraced buildings standing parallel to the market stalls. [Richard Green]

Helen and Pat's china and glassware stall is a browser's and collector's dream. [Richard Green]

Richard Carter's fine display of picture frames. [Richard Green]

George's boot and shoe stall, always full of various styles of footwear. [Richard Green]

Bag Lady and chairman of the Wells Chamber of Commerce, Cheryl Carter is a staunch advocate for the market traders. [Richard Green]

Crowds throng around 'Kathleen', the former Stokes's family traction engine. [Richard Green]

Wells was now going through some of the biggest transformations in its long history. If mistakes were made in the process of 'enhancing' the Market Place, the city's other much talked-about topic (for more than 60 years!) was the need for a relief road to save the ancient townscape.

Against this background, Alan Cooper of the Wells Civic Society rightly commented that 'Wells has to be the most public-consulted city in Somerset.' A public seminar was held in 1993, 'A Vision for Wells', and from then on public consultation was the order of the day.

The 1993 November Carnival Charter Fair got off to a flying start with a revival of the civic opening ceremony, when all the local top brass assembled in Wells Town Hall. 'Oyez! Oyez! Oyez!' bellowed Fred Gibbons, the Town Crier, after leading out the guests from the Town Hall, introducing showman Joey Stokes to make the opening speech, followed by the Mayor, Councillor Kate Fry. It was then a ride on the Dodgems, when of all people Albert Heal, making a welcome return, had trouble starting his car!

After a tour of the Fair, the guests returned to the Mayor's Parlour for more speeches and refreshments.

A month later, the 'Vision for Wells' seminar was held in the Bishop Bradfield Rooms of the Old Deanery, with the purpose of encouraging 'a better understanding of the thoughts and feelings of interested groups in the city, so that these may be taken into account when formulating our future.' This meeting was a watershed, presaging very welcome public consultation on future matters of concern to the citizens of England's smallest city.

The most appropriate 'sound bite' to come out of the day-long meeting was from the seminar chairman, Richard Guise:

> There aren't many towns and cities that still have fairs, right in the Market Place. This is a direct tie back to the history of the city – it is not a screw-on heritage bit. Long may it live!

It was now recognised that the use of the Market Place was the key to a successful future.

In the following year, there was for the first time ever a 'Freedom of the Fair', an hour of free rides and refreshments, courtesy of Joey Stokes and fellow showmen, for all local 'special needs' citizens. That year's souvenir brochure, which also went out to local schools, went straight to the heart of the matter:

> The Market Place has been, and always will be, a topical subject, but with a little thought, some common sense and a bit of entrepreneurial spirit among shopkeepers, hoteliers, market operators and the Showmen's Guild, with support from the Councils and other organisations (all working together), the heart of the city can still share a long-

standing tradition, which in turn is an integral part of the customs and ceremonies, and a living heritage of Britain.

By May, 1995 major repair work was needed to the newly enhanced Market Place, where the stone setts were causing a problem. It seemed the enhancements had not been designed to take heavy traffic. Local shopkeepers were up in arms, pointing out that they had given their forecasts of traffic needs, and that the Fair should also have been taken into account. Peter Wicks on their behalf asked how much the exercise would cost and who would foot the bill?

Meanwhile debate continued to rage about the future siting of the Fairs. 'Complaints Put Future of Annual City Fair in Doubt' headlined the *Western Gazette*, a month after the showmen had left, and there was a petition for the fairs to be removed either to the Recreation Ground or the Prince's Road/Market Street car park. The paper followed up the following week, reporting, 'It's swings and roundabouts over support for the moving of the twice-yearly funfairs from the Market Place'. Wells Town Clerk Keith Donoghue argued that 'there is inadequate supervision of setting up, the noise, and notification to neighbours.' Some councillors asked about the feasibility of alternative sites, while Councillor Norman Kennedy took a pragmatic view: 'I would like to see it stay in the Market Place, although it should be better monitored. The size of the rides should also be monitored as there is so much high-tech equipment about.'

The Father of the City Council, Councillor Harry Parkes, was opposed to a move to the Recreation Ground: 'It would quickly become a mire or a bog . . . As I understand it, the ancient Charters give rights to fairs anywhere in the city. The deed which allowed the Town Hall to be built gives a right for a fair to be held within its former curtilage.'

A third article in the *Western Gazette* proclaimed, 'Fun Fairs to stay in Market Place', with Councillor John Gibson arguing that the events were occasions when the city sprang to life, while Councillor Rosemary Woods added, 'Wells has a long tradition of Fairs in the Market Place. It is more a problem of policing them than a need to stop them. To remove them will cause other problems.'

1995 also saw the Market Place enhancements earn a prestigious Civic Trust award.

Thursday November 9th saw the third revived opening ceremony and showman Joey Stokes was presented with a wooden plaque bearing the City of Wells coat of arms in recognition of his devotion to the city's heritage.

Helping in the build-up to the 700th anniversary, businessman and City Councillor Fred Wilcox of West Country Fairs helped the present author to put together a Wells Carnival Fair Painting Competition involving some local schools for the 1996 Charter Fair.

Ready for the 1993 May Fair 'pull on' with the Stokes's family fleet of transport in Chamberlain Street car park; and coming down Sadler Street, the slow moving convoy of the Cole family's transport about to enter the Market Place for the 2000 May Charter Fair. [Richard Green]

76

Wiltshire showman James Jennings arriving with his Dodgems for the Carnival Charter Fair in 1984. [Alan Southwood]; and just after 8 am on Thursday, April 29th, 1993: Joey Stokes is the first showman to set up on the raised area of the first phase of the new 'enhanced' Market Place. [Richard Green]

All hands are needed to help Joey Stokes get the Dodgem roof in place for the 1993 May Fair; and mighty sized Meccano! The Cole family's Dodgem track, seen here in 2000, dates back to the 1930s. [Richard Green]

Joseph Stokes helps unload the Dodgem cars at the 1993 May Fair. [Richard Green]

So often overlooked by the media: the many hours of free rides for special needs citizens. [Richard Green]

Showman Albert Heal stands by the Mayor of Wells, Councillor Kate Fry at the first official opening ceremony, with Town Crier Fred Gibbons and City Macebearer Gil Weatherhead in the Mayor's Parlour during the 1993 November Carnival Charter Fair. [Richard Green]

Ready to ride showman Charles Appleton's Miami at the 1994 November fair are Town Clerk, Keith Donoghue, Wells Tourism Chairman, Ian Poynter, Councillors Christina Baron and Norman Kennedy and other dignitaries. [Richard Green]

Spot Town Clerk, Keith Donoghue and Mayor of Wells, Councillor John Howett on Charles Smith's stall at the 1994 November fair. [Richard Green]

Town Crier, Fred Gibbons poses with the Mayor, Councillor Nicholas Denison at the 1995 November Fair. [Ernie Taylor]

Charter Fair regular, John Nail and family with his huge 'Pick'. [Ernie Taylor]

At the November, 1995 Fair: standing far right is the late Father of Wells City Council, Councillor Harry Parkes, whose tireless support for the fairs and markets to be held in the Market Place should never be forgotten. [Richard Green]

To mark the showmen's devotion to the city's heritage, Councillor Nicholas Denison, the Mayor of Wells, presents Joey Stokes with a wooden shield, bearing the city's crest, at the 1995 Carnival Charter Fair. [Ernie Taylor]

J STOKES & SONS AMUSEMENTS

(Members of the Showmen's Guild of Great Britain)

CARNIVAL FAIR

(The 698th Year of Charter Fairs)

OPEN THURSDAY 14th and FRIDAY 15th NOVEMBER

Come and see

THE OFFICIAL OPENING CEREMONY

(on the steps of J Stokes & Sons Dodgems)

To be opened by the Guest of Honour, The Mayor of the City of Wells, Councillor Isobel Marshall

Thursday, 14th November at 5 pm

Preceded by

THE FREEDOM OF THE FAIR

for our invited guests: local special needs people starting at 4 pm

NEW THIS YEAR: CHARTER FAIR PAINTING COMPETITION

(Mr J Stokes would like to thank all those who helped with the various events)

The 1996 Fair Painting Competition: Mayor, Councillor Isobel Marshall, the Mayor's Mace Bearer, Gil Weatherhead and main sponsor, Fred Wilcox, renowned for his Town Hall markets, with winners Wells Central Junior School. [Richard Green]

. . . and with competition winner, Miranda Pepe. [Richard Green]

The Mayor, Councillor Roy MacKenzie and Mayoress Jane MacKenzie at the 1997 November Carnival Charter Fair, watched by Councillors Rosemary Woods and Maureen Brandon, both of whom would undertake later opening ceremonies; and one of Councillor Roy MacKenzie's hidden talents is that he is an air rifle shooting instructor: seen here at the 1997 November Fair. [Richard Green]

Photo-call for the preview of the Wells Charter Fair Tapestry, 1997. [Richard Green]

The fair was widely publicised in the media, with a live early-morning broadcast on BBC Somerset Sound for the Mayor, Councillor Isobel Marshall, before going to Stoberry Park School to present prizes and gifts, with later presentations at the Wells Central School and another live broadcast on BBC Radio Bristol. At 4 o'clock it was 'Freedom of the Fair' for people with special needs, assisted by the City of Wells Lions and the St. John Ambulance, with the Opening Ceremony following, along with yet another live broadcast on BBC Somerset Sound.

During 1996 and 1997, the 700th Anniversary Charter Fair Tapestry was created by no fewer than eight local schools. The 1200s were represented by St. Joseph and St. Theresa School of Wells; the 1300s by Priddy School; the 1400s by Wells Stoberry Park Junior School; the 1500s by Westbury-sub-Mendip St Lawrence School; the 1600s by Chewton Mendip Primary School; the 1700s by Horrington School; the 1800s by the Wells Blue School, and the 1900s by Wells Stoberry Park Infants School.

The very impressive tapestry – measuring two feet wide by 30 feet long and using a multi-media of materials, ranging from calligraphy to collage – made its debut at the 1997 November Fair.

But 1997 was also eventful in less happy ways. There was a dispute between showmen Charles Heal and Joey Stokes, which raised again the question of the future of the Fairs in the Market Place. The *Wells Journal* reported on its front page:

> Many of the Fair rides had not been erected because of a dispute between rival operators. Charles Heal and Sons obtained County Court permission to mount this year's Fair, but Joey Stokes, who has run the Fair for the last few years, also turned up and had to leave his trailers in a nearby car park. A spokeswoman for the Showmen's Guild of Great Britain said that Joey Stokes was appealing against the decision and apologised to fair-goers for the lack of rides.

This unfortunate incident gave ammunition to those who wanted to see the Fairs removed permanently from the Market Place. Respected Market Place antique dealer, Edward Nowell commented that 'perhaps the time has come for the Charters to be forgotten and the Fair moved elsewhere?' Ernie Taylor, the *World's Fair* reporter, wrote: 'I would have thought that this was the smallest May Fair this century, but veteran fairground enthusiast and local businessman, Alan Southwood, assured me that it was not. Alan can remember occasions during the last War when the lessee, the late Charles Heal, erected three hoop-las, in order to safeguard the Charter.'

Celebrating their 650th anniversary, Priddy Sheep Fair, up on the Mendips, also had problems, but of their own making – crowds and livestock on the

Lower Green reaching saturation point! A referendum produced just 16 votes in favour of discontinuing the Fair, while 135 wanted it to continue as it was, and 149 wanted some changes.

The following six months again saw a dispute at the November Fair, and only tough negotiations between Joseph Stokes, Charles Heal and the Town Clerk, Keith Donoghue prevented a disaster, with the *Wells Journal* reporting, 'Fair Operators negotiate a way out of long-running dispute'.

CHAPTER 6

'The Show Must Go On'

The troubled events of 1997 were, happily, to prove a turning point, for lessons were learnt and positive ideas formulated. As ever, the *World's Fair* reporter, Ernie Taylor, put it succinctly in his article, 'All Goes Well at Civic Opening'.

For the first time, a senior Showmen's Guild official attended the opening ceremony, in the person of their vice-chairman, Ramon Henderson. Mr Henderson publicly thanked the Mayor and colleagues, particularly Town Clerk Keith Donoghue, for their efforts in keeping the Fair where it belonged, in the Market Place.

The 700th Anniversary Charter Fair Tapestry made its debut in a ceremony attended by dignitaries, special guests and representatives of the participating schools.

Despite all the goodwill built up by so many people, there were still calls for the Fair to be removed from the Market Place. The ever faithful *Wells Journal* yet again recorded the continuing saga in a piece entitled 'Historic Fair Under Threat'. Councillor John Howett was quoted as calling for the Fair to be removed to the Chamberlain Street car park, which would allow operators to offer bigger rides. Former businessman and Wellensian, Alan Southwood spoke for all those who wanted to keep the status quo: 'the Fair is one of the traditions Wells should not lose.'

At a crucial meeting of the Council, only one councillor wanted the Charter Fairs removed, and no resolution was put forward, allowing the press to report 'Traders Fail to Move Fair'. Meanwhile, positive steps were taken to improve safety, with future licences being conditional on strict observance of Health and Safety guidelines, test and insurance certificates. The fair operators guaranteed full co-operation in these matters.

Immense local publicity heralded the coming of the 700th Anniversary, with a series of three articles in the *Wells Journal*, as well as a major double-page spread in the *World's Fair* and special limited edition souvenir brochures which were distributed to local schools. The Fair Tapestry was proudly displayed in the Wells Museum.

Flanked by showmen Monty Hammond and Owen Smith, Charles Heal holds the 1947 Carnival Cup which the family firm donated to the city, with the 1998 Western Section Showmen's Guild chairman, Ramon Henderson. [Ernie Taylor]; and a proud moment for showman Charles Heal as Mayor of Wells, Councillor Rosemary Woods presents him with a 700th anniversary cake as a surprise gift. The family have presented over 150 fairs between 1900 and 2000. [Richard Green]

Thursday November 12th, 1998 was the big day, starting at four o'clock with an hour of the now traditional free rides for those with special needs, courtesy of the showmen, with among the team leaders representing their various organisations, Ivy Flagg for Wookey, Jessie Henderson for Street, Bob Freebury and Sarah Curnow for Cheddar and Wookey, and Jane Doble for Street and Wells.

Sadly, one special guest was missing at the opening ceremony – the ever popular Town Crier, Fred Gibbons, who was ill – and the present author was given the privilege of leading out the distinguished guests to the steps of Monty Hammond's set of Dodgems.

Part of the opening ceremonials was a surprise presentation to Charles Heal of a 700th Anniversary cake, which had been especially made by Nancy Dodd, secretary of the Wells Carnival Committee. Handing over the delightful cake, coated in white icing with a miniature roundabout on top, the Mayor, Councillor Rosemary Woods, thanked Charles Heal for everything he had done for the city, saying 'I hope that Wells will retain its Market Place Fairs for at least another 700 years!'

Making up the 700th fair were Monty Hammond's Dodgems and Orbiter, Charles Appleton's Miami, with games from John Smith Jnr, Thomas Stevens, Paul Lucas, John Nail and James R. Rawlings, and kiosks by Denise Lucas, Steven Fullwood, Monty Hammond, George Symonds, Monty Howell and J.R. Rawlings.

If 1998 finished on a high note, the following year was to hit yet another low, with the *Wells Journal* reporting a 'Debate on Details of Fair Rental Dispute: Operator Unwilling to Pay More to Council'. This was sparked by a proposal to increase the rent from £583 to £1,000 per Fair. The sensible approach was suggested by Bill McKay, then Chairman of Mendip District Council, who called for someone to mediate to ensure a 'fair deal for Wells'.

Looking back over all these years of controversy, it is perhaps amazing how the Fairs and Markets have survived. One recurring criticism that needs to be answered is that 'It's the same Fair every year'. The reality is that in the period from 1985 to 1999, the Charter Fairs saw over 30 different rides and attractions, and for the record, it is interesting to list them: six different sets of Dodgems, six different Waltzers, three different Miamis, three different Orbiters, three different Round-Ups, two different Big Wheels, two different Fun Houses, two different Trabants, two different Glass Houses, along with one each of Ghost Train, Looper, Twist, Matterhorn, Rock-O-Plane, Super Trooper and Tip-Top, as well as a vast number of different side and round stalls.

And behind the image of 'all the fun of the fair' are the realities of business life: ever increasing costs, the change over to silent running generators, staff to be paid, spiralling transport costs of fuel and tax, and changing legislation in the areas of food safety and health and safety rules covering rides and attractions.

This is all to be set against the background of the growth in competing leisure pursuits, ranging from theme parks – many with fair-related attractions – to the information technology of press-button 'virtual reality'. So the threat to the living traditions of the Charter Fairs has never been greater.

It has been well said that a Fair is like a chameleon, constantly changing to new situations and trends, and thankfully for Wells the mediator in the rent dispute came down in favour of Charles Heal.

So what, now, should be the attractions of the last May Charter Fair of the decade, of the last century of the last one thousand years?

In keeping with the true showmanship of surprise, Hampshire showmen Billy and Peter Cole made not only their first visit to Wells, but also to Somerset. The Cole family's Miami made up the nucleus of the very colourful fair. In a sad reflection of the modern world, but emphasising the family character of the event, the showmen erected notices prohibiting alcohol and drugs.

The last year of the century was a poignant one, and with togetherness and family values being more and more highlighted, Michael Chamberlain, a preacher for St Cuthbert's Church of Wells and for Fletcher House Chapel in the city, wrote a 'Sermon of the Week' for the *Western Daily Press*:

> Hundreds of people visited the Mid-Somerset Show at Shepton Mallet yesterday. Thousands will be in the Mendip top village of Priddy on Wednesday for the annual Sheep Fair.
>
> Both events are times and opportunities in the calendar, when town and country come together to appreciate the creation.
>
> On Wednesday, millions watched the Eclipse across the world. Nothing man-made about such an historic event but, again, all part of the creation.
>
> To whom should we attribute this creation? The answer is, of course, in the Old Testament. God made the heavens and the earth and all that is in them.
>
> It is therefore our duty as custodians to learn about them, educate others about them, and to hand them on for a future generation to enjoy.

There was another show of togetherness at the November Carnival Charter Fair on Thursday November 11th, 1999, for it was also Armistice Day and the showmen joined in the two-minute silence around the Fountain entrance to the Fair: an observation broadcast on a BBC Radio programme put together by the Town Clerk, Keith Donoghue.

Pausing during a Health and Safety inspection are showman Charles Heal and Town Clerk Keith Donoghue at the May Charter Fair, 1999. [Richard Green]

Sign of the times at the May Charter Fair, 1999. [Richard Green]

MEMBERS OF THE SHOWMENS GUILD OF GREAT BRITAIN

CHARLES HEAL AND SONS

(EST. 1881)

PRESENTS

CARNIVAL CHARTER FAIR

WELLS MARKET PLACE
11th and 12th November

with

All the latest fairground rides and attractions

OFFICIAL CIVIC OPENING CEREMONY

with guest of honour

The Mayor of the City of Wells: Cllr Maureen Brandon

With Special Guests

FROM SOMERSET'S REMAINING CHARTER FAIR TOWNS

at 5.00 pm on Thursday, 12th November,
at the Dodgems
followed by

'THE FREEDOM OF THE FAIR'
FOR SPECIAL NEEDS PEOPLE

Kindly assisted by St John Ambulance and Wells Lions

*MR CHARLES HEAL, WOULD LIKE TO THANK ALL WHO HELPED
WITH THE VARIOUS EVENTS*

Photocall for the Mayor of Wells, the Junior Mayor of Wells and the Town Crier, Les Long, at the 1999 November Fair. [Richard Green]

99

A rare shot of the Carnival Fair before the crowds arrive: numbers can range from 20,000 to 50,000 depending on the weather. [Richard Green]

Showman Monty Hammond (left) and the author with the Mayor of Wells, Councillor Maureen Brandon. [Stuart Beese]

The Mayor's Consort, Alistair Glanville gives the Mayor, Councillor Maureen Brandon and Junior Mayor, Lydia Walsh a helping hand, as they prepare for a ride on Monty Hammond's Orbiter at the 1999 November Fair. [Richard Green]

Six hours later, at five o'clock the author was privileged to lead out a very special delegation of mayors and civic leaders for the official civic opening ceremony, for the evening was to 'Celebrate 1000 years of Somerset Charter Fairs', with delegates from Axbridge, Chard, Crewkerne, Glastonbury, Ilminster, Priddy, Shepton Mallet, Street and Weston-super-Mare.

Following the author, was the new Town Crier, Les Long, who was also President of the Wells Carnival Committee; along with the Mayor of Wells, Councillor Maureen Brandon and her Consort, Alistair Glanville; the Deputy Mayor, Desmond Gripper, with the Serjeant at Mace to the Mayor, Gill Weatherhead who this year was also the Prime Warden of Macebearers; and the Serjeant at Mace to the City Council, John Harris, followed by several City Councillors.

Other notables in attendance included the Wells Cathedral Administrator, John Roberts and his wife; the Freeman of Wells and Carnival Secretary, Nancy Dodd; along with the Carnival Princess, Sally Cooper and her attendants, Natalie Carter, Mandy Cooper, Jasmine Gray and Samantha Millican.

Representing the City of Wells Lions was Alf Orriss, and special needs were represented by Stuart Beese, while for the St John Ambulance Brigade the representative was Divisional Superintendent Gerald Woods; for Avon and Somerset Constabulary, the recently appointed Inspector Dennis Harries; and also in attendance were the head boys and head girls of the Wells Blue School and the Wells Cathedral School. Alan and Margaret Southwood represented the Fairground Association of Great Britain.

Supporting the Mayor of Wells throughout the evening was the Junior Mayor of Wells, Lydia Walsh.

As we move into the new century, it is perhaps salutary to remind ourselves of an aspect of the Market Fairs that all good-thinking townsfolk of Wells would roundly deplore: the element of unpleasant antagonism towards both market traders and showmen – well summed up by Cheryl Carter, both market trader and at the time Chairman of Wells Chamber of Commerce: 'We are sometimes treated like second-class citizens who live on camp sites . . . We work very hard and are proud to uphold the centuries-old tradition of market trading.' As the Right Reverend, the Bishop of Bath and Wells, James Thompson (Bishop Jim) has put it: 'We all need the capacity to understand each other.'

To this end, I hope this book has given a better understanding of the Wells Charter Fairs and Markets. Despite all the ups and downs, it is so important that their historic legacy and heritage are upheld and that 'The Show Must Go On!'

Ever diligent, reporter Ernie Taylor summed up his 1999 visit: 'I was fortunate to be invited to the reception, following the official opening of the Wells Carnival Fair. Showman Monty Hammond, standing in for Charles Heal, did a fine job,

Hampshire showman, Billy Cole holds the tape for the 2000 May
Charter Fair. [Richard Green]

103

All smiles as the Health and Safety inspection is completed by Charles Heal and Town Clerk Keith Donoghue, May 2000. [Richard Green]

Cheryl Carter, Chairman of the Wells Chamber of Commerce, with showman Charles Heal at the 2000 May Charter Fair. A trader herself, Cheryl is often found at the twice-weekly markets. [Richard Green]

A rare view from the Town Hall. [Richard Green]

The next generation of showmen to keep the charter fairs alive! [Ernie Taylor]

mixing with the Civic dignitaries and explaining all aspects of the business. It is through such contacts that the image of our Fairs will be improved in the corridors of power, where some elected officers are not always sympathetic.'

It was fitting that Saturday September 8th, 2001, the 800th anniversary of the signing of the first Royal Charter, should be celebrated along with the 550th anniversary of Thomas Beckington, the Bishop of Bath and Wells' letters patent for the construction of the original conduit of September 1451 which gave the city a cleaner and improved environment: surely a unique double celebration.

As the century turned into the year 2000, both the Charter Fairs and Markets were still making the headlines in the *Wells Journal*: 'Chaos at Market as Stalls Fail to Arrive – Sabotage Claim by Traders on Firm's Final Day of Management'. It was a problem – not helped by persistent showers – of staff not arriving to put up stalls on the last day under the management of R and C Markets.

Mendip District Council's Greg King, the councillor responsible for the Markets, was reported as saying:

> Last-minute efforts by stallholders saved the day when stall erectors contracted to market operators R and C failed to turn up. Saturday was the last day for R and C before new market operators MIL take over the contract. This is a stupid and irresponsible act by the stall erectors and has damaged the livelihood of many stallholders who depend on trade in Wells.
>
> . . . Since winning the contract MIL have met with stallholders and I am encouraged by the positive response. The retail industry is undergoing major changes. Local markets have to adapt to survive and I look forward to a fresh start in all the markets in Mendip, with new ideas, more publicity and more local people using them.

The same issue of the *Journal* carried another story about the long-running dispute between Charles Heal and Sons and the Stokes family, which was finally nearing its end, after years of lengthy legal battles in and out of the courts.

Councillors agreed to let the 2000 May Charter Fair to Charles Heal, who along with any other interested operator was now invited to tender to hold the historic fair for a three-year contract. As this book has shown, apart from the two world wars, Charles Heal and Sons have held court in the Wells Market Place since 1908, and from the 1920s an almost unbroken 30 years of benefit nights for the Wells and District Cottage Hospital, with the proceeds helping towards an extension to the hospital. Charles Heal was also a great benefactor to the Wells Carnival, donating silverware still in use today. The Heal family, while holding on to its historical traditions, has done much to create a modern family fun fair, and enjoy a good reputation with many local councils.

'THE SHOW MUST GO ON'

An extract from Mary Hobbs' 1957 article in the *Wells Journal* concludes this survey of centuries of markets and fairs in this fair city of Wells:

> . . . Dusk falls and the traders pack up and retire. The last rushlight is put out, and the town is quiet, save for the watchman's 'All's well', until at cock-crow, the next Fair-Day begins.

I blame my interest on my father. I have upheld his fascination with the fair. Is this the new generation to keep the interest going? [Richard Green]